HAL•LEONARD

pro vocal®
BETTER THAN KARAOKE!

SONGBOOK & SOUND-ALIKE CD
WITH UNIQUE *PITCH-CHANGER*™

SONGS
Children
CAN SING!

BOYS AND GIRLS EDITION
VOLUME 1

TO101590

ISBN 978-1-4584-2367-2

HAL•LEONARD®
CORPORATION

7777 W. BLUEMOUND RD. P.O. BOX 13819 MILWAUKEE, WI 53213

Visit Hal Leonard Online at
www.halleonard.com

Getting to Know You

from THE KING AND I
Lyrics by Oscar Hammerstein II
Music by Richard Rodgers

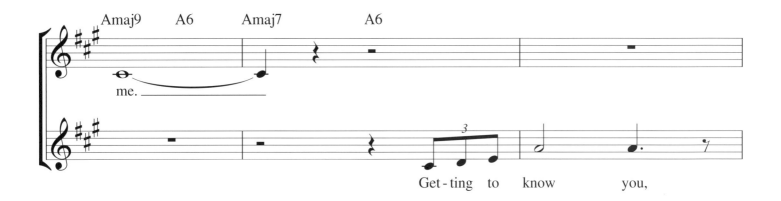

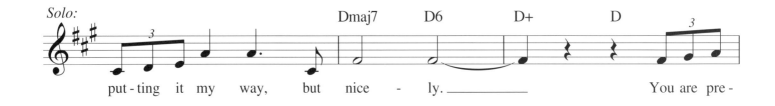

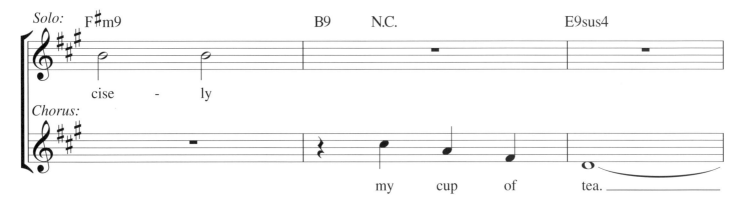

Happy Talk

from SOUTH PACIFIC
Lyrics by Oscar Hammerstein II
Music by Richard Rodgers

I Whistle a Happy Tune

from THE KING AND I
Lyrics by Oscar Hammerstein II
Music by Richard Rodgers

vinc - es me that I'm not a - fraid.

%. Bridge 2

Make be - lieve you're brave, and the

trip will take you far. You may be as

brave as you make be - lieve you are.

You may be as brave

as you make be - lieve you are. _____

My Favorite Things

from THE SOUND OF MUSIC
Lyrics by Oscar Hammerstein II
Music by Richard Rodgers

crisp ap - ple stru - dels, door-bells and sleigh-bells and
schnit - zels with noo - dles, wild geese that fly with the
moon on their wings, these are a few of my
fa - vor - ite things.

Verse

Girls in white dress - es with blue sat - in sash - es,
snow - flakes that stay on my nose and eye - lash - es,
sil - ver white win - ters that melt in - to springs,

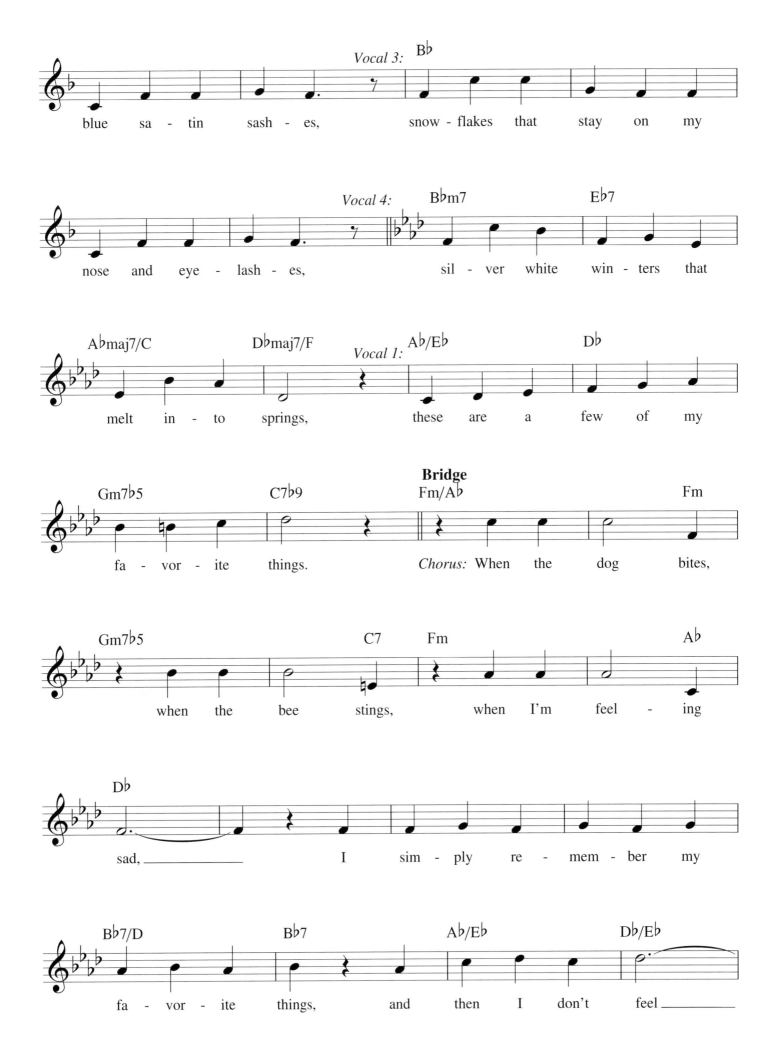

The Sound of Music

from THE SOUND OF MUSIC
Lyrics by Oscar Hammerstein II
Music by Richard Rodgers

with the sound of mu - sic, _____ and I'll

sing once more. _____

Interlude

Chorus: Ooh, _____ ooh. _____

_____ To

laugh like a brook when it trips and falls o - ver stones on its

way, _____ to sing through the night like a

lark who is learn - ing to pray. I go to the hills _____

Take Me Out to the Ball Game

Words by Jack Norworth
Music by Albert von Tilzer

Coda I

Verse 2

This Land Is Your Land

Words and Music by Woody Guthrie

Outro

from Cal - i - for - nia _____ to the New York is - land,

from the Red - wood For - est _____ to the Gulf Stream wa - ters. _____

_____ This land was made for you and me. _____

_____ This land was made for you and me. _____

_____ This land _____ was made

for you and me, _____

_____ made for you and me, _____

_____ for you and me.

Tomorrow

from the Musical Production ANNIE
Lyric by Martin Charnin
Music by Charles Strouse

chin and grin and ___ say, ___ "Oh." ___ The

Chorus

sun -'ll come out ___ to - mor - row, ___ so ya got - ta hang on 'til to -

mor - row, ___ come what may. To -

mor - row, to - mor - row, I love ya, to - mor - row, you're

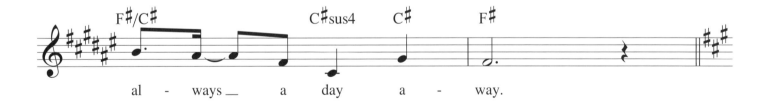
al - ways ___ a day a - way.

Bridge

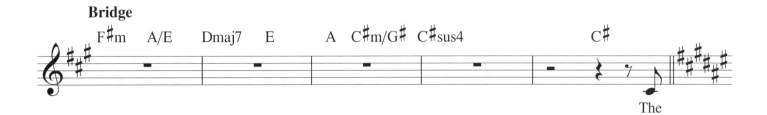
The

38

Chorus

sun-'ll come out _____ to-mor-row, _____ so ya got-ta hang on 'til to-

mor - row, _____ come what may. To -

mor-row, to-mor-row, I love ya, to-mor-row, you're

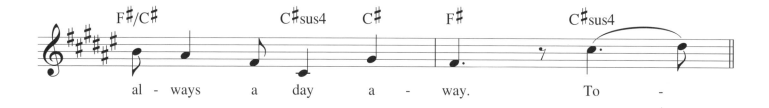

al - ways a day a - way. To -

Outro

mor-row, to-mor-row, I love ya, to-mor-row, you're al - ways _ a

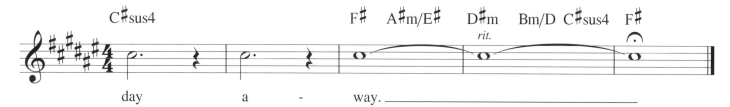

day a - way. _____

Pro Vocal® Series

SONGBOOK & SOUND-ALIKE CD
SING 8 GREAT SONGS
WITH A PROFESSIONAL BAND

Whether you're a karaoke singer or an auditioning professional, the Pro Vocal® series is for you! Unlike most karaoke packs, each book in the Pro Vocal Series contains the lyrics, melody, and chord symbols for eight hit songs. The CD contains demos for listening, and separate backing tracks so you can sing along. The CD is playable on any CD player, but it is also enhanced so PC and Mac computer users can adjust the recording to any pitch without changing the tempo! Perfect for home rehearsal, parties, auditions, corporate events, and gigs without a backup band.

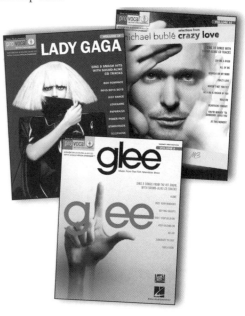

WOMEN'S EDITIONS

00740247	1. Broadway Songs	$14.95
00740249	2. Jazz Standards	$15.99
00740246	3. Contemporary Hits	$14.95
00740277	4. '80s Gold	$12.95
00740299	5. Christmas Standards	$15.95
00740281	6. Disco Fever	$12.95
00740279	7. R&B Super Hits	$12.95
00740309	8. Wedding Gems	$12.95
00740409	9. Broadway Standards	$14.95
00740348	10. Andrew Lloyd Webber	$14.95
00740344	11. Disney's Best	$15.99
00740378	12. Ella Fitzgerald	$14.95
00740350	14. Musicals of Boublil & Schönberg	$14.95
00740377	15. Kelly Clarkson	$14.95
00740342	16. Disney Favorites	$15.99
00740353	17. Jazz Ballads	$14.99
00740376	18. Jazz Vocal Standards	$16.99
00740375	20. Hannah Montana	$16.95
00740354	21. Jazz Favorites	$14.99
00740374	22. Patsy Cline	$14.95
00740369	23. Grease	$14.95
00740367	25. ABBA	$15.99
00740365	26. Movie Songs	$14.95
00740360	28. High School Musical 1 & 2	$14.95
00740363	29. Torch Songs	$14.95
00740379	30. Hairspray	$15.99
00740380	31. Top Hits	$14.95
00740384	32. Hits of the '70s	$14.95
00740388	33. Billie Holiday	$14.95
00740389	34. The Sound of Music	$16.99
00740390	35. Contemporary Christian	$14.95
00740392	36. Wicked	$16.99
00740393	37. More Hannah Montana	$14.95
00740394	38. Miley Cyrus	$14.95
00740396	39. Christmas Hits	$15.95
00740410	40. Broadway Classics	$14.95
00740415	41. Broadway Favorites	$14.99
00740416	42. Great Standards You Can Sing	$14.99
00740417	43. Singable Standards	$14.99
00740418	44. Favorite Standards	$14.99
00740419	45. Sing Broadway	$14.99
00740420	46. More Standards	$14.99
00740421	47. Timeless Hits	$14.99
00740422	48. Easygoing R&B	$14.99
00740424	49. Taylor Swift	$16.99
00740425	50. From This Moment On	$14.99
00740426	51. Great Standards Collection	$19.99
00740430	52. Worship Favorites	$14.99
00740434	53. Lullabyes	$14.99
00740438	54. Lady Gaga	$14.99
00740444	55. Amy Winehouse	$15.99
00740445	56. Adele	$14.99
00740446	57. The Grammy Awards Best Female Pop Vocal Performance 1990-1999	$14.99
00740447	58. The Grammy Awards Best Female Pop Vocal Performance 2000-2009	$14.99

MEN'S EDITIONS

00740248	1. Broadway Songs	$14.95
00740250	2. Jazz Standards	$14.95
00740251	3. Contemporary Hits	$14.99
00740278	4. '80s Gold	$12.95
00740298	5. Christmas Standards	$15.95
00740280	6. R&B Super Hits	$12.95
00740282	7. Disco Fever	$12.95
00740310	8. Wedding Gems	$12.95
00740411	9. Broadway Greats	$14.99
00740333	10. Elvis Presley – Volume 1	$14.95
00740349	11. Andrew Lloyd Webber	$14.95
00740345	12. Disney's Best	$14.95
00740347	13. Frank Sinatra Classics	$14.95
00740334	14. Lennon & McCartney	$14.99
00740335	16. Elvis Presley – Volume 2	$14.99
00740343	17. Disney Favorites	$14.99
00740351	18. Musicals of Boublil & Schönberg	$14.95
00740337	19. Lennon & McCartney – Volume 2	$14.99
00740346	20. Frank Sinatra Standards	$14.95
00740338	21. Lennon & McCartney – Volume 3	$14.95
00740358	22. Great Standards	$14.99
00740336	23. Elvis Presley	$14.99
00740341	24. Duke Ellington	$14.99
00740339	25. Lennon & McCartney – Volume 4	$14.95
00740359	26. Pop Standards	$14.99
00740362	27. Michael Bublé	$15.99
00740364	29. Torch Songs	$14.95
00740366	30. Movie Songs	$14.95
00740368	31. Hip Hop Hits	$14.95
00740370	32. Grease	$14.95
00740371	33. Josh Groban	$14.95
00740373	34. Billy Joel	$14.99
00740381	35. Hits of the '50s	$14.95
00740382	36. Hits of the '60s	$14.95
00740383	37. Hits of the '70s	$14.95
00740385	38. Motown	$14.95
00740386	39. Hank Williams	$14.95
00740387	40. Neil Diamond	$14.95
00740391	41. Contemporary Christian	$14.95
00740397	42. Christmas Hits	$15.95
00740399	43. Ray	$14.95
00740400	44. The Rat Pack Hits	$14.99
00740401	45. Songs in the Style of Nat "King" Cole	$14.99
00740402	46. At the Lounge	$14.95
00740403	47. The Big Band Singer	$14.95
00740404	48. Jazz Cabaret Songs	$14.99
00740405	49. Cabaret Songs	$14.99
00740406	50. Big Band Standards	$14.99
00740412	51. Broadway's Best	$14.99
00740427	52. Great Standards Collection	$19.99
00740431	53. Worship Favorites	$14.99
00740435	54. Barry Manilow	$14.99
00740436	55. Lionel Richie	$14.99
00740439	56. Michael Bublé – Crazy Love	$15.99
00740441	57. Johnny Cash	$14.99
00740442	58. Bruno Mars	$14.99
00740448	59. The Grammy Awards Best Male Pop Vocal Performance 1990-1999	$14.99
00740449	60. The Grammy Awards Best Male Pop Vocal Performance 2000-2009	$14.99

MIXED EDITIONS

These editions feature songs for both male and female voices.

00740311	1. Wedding Duets	$12.95
00740398	2. Enchanted	$14.95
00740407	3. Rent	$14.95
00740408	4. Broadway Favorites	$14.99
00740413	5. South Pacific	$15.99
00740414	6. High School Musical 3	$14.99
00740429	7. Christmas Carols	$14.99
00740437	8. Glee	$16.99
00740440	9. More Songs from Glee	$21.99
00740443	10. Even More Songs from Glee	$15.99

Visit Hal Leonard online at
www.halleonard.com

7777 W. BLUEMOUND RD. P.O. BOX 13819 MILWAUKEE, WI 53213

Prices, contents, & availability subject to change without notice.

0112